Asit Maitra

Knife on the Edge

Biscuit Publishing

First published 2010 by
Biscuit Publishing Ltd
PO Box 123
Washington
NE37 2YW
United Kingdom

www.biscuitpublishing.com

ISBN   978 1 903914 41 0

Typeset by Free Spirit Writers, Bridlington

Acknowledgements

Numbers (Other Poetry, 2002), Trapped (Other Poetry, 2003), A Bangladeshi corner shopkeeper (Norwich OPC Anthology, 2004), Going to England (renamed Saraswati's Blessing in Chapati-Moon, ID on Tyne Press, 2007), The Face (Sun Dips at Juhu Beach, Biscuit Publishing, 2009) and Two Lives (Book of Ten, Zebra Publishing, 2009).

The author would like to thank Brian Lister of Biscuit Publishing for keeping faith with his school of writers, and publishing this author's second full-length collection. Also to the teachers of Creative Writing, School Of English, University of Newcastle, with special thanks to Cynthia Fuller and Gillian Allnutt for their valuable contributions. To Pam Lack for the cover photography and feedback, and Adrian, Jess and Anita for their encouragement and support.

Asit Maitra, FRCS, Emeritus A&E consultant (Newcastle Hospitals NHS Foundation Trust), MA (Creative Writing, Newcastle University), came to Britain from India in 1961 and has lived in Newcastle since 1977. This is his second full-length collection, having published chapbooks – Zig-Zags (with Pat Borthwick), Pharos Press, 1998, and Chapati-moon, ID on Tyne Press, 2007, and first full-length collection – Sun Dips at Juhu Beach, Biscuit Publishing, 2009.

His poems have been published in Acumen, Other poetry, Dream Catcher, Norwich OPC Anthologies, Blinking Eye OPC Anthologies, Redbeck Anthology of South Asian Poetry, 2000 and Masala – Poetry from India, Bangladesh, Pakistan & Sri Lanka, Macmillan's Children Book, 2005, Both sides of the Hadrian's Wall, 2006, Book of Ten, Zebra Publishing, 2009.

For late Mrs Sudhanshu Maitra

The idea for this collection came while the writer was on a holiday. He decided to write a page each day recollecting scenes from the past, here in England, that flashed back spontaneously. The first twenty-one poems paint a picture of a young immigrant with a dream, his journey, and the consequences in loosely connected but independent episodes. The reader is drawn into the drama of hospital life, elation and heart-breaks.

Other poems have been written at different times touching on medical themes and a wide variety of topics from emotional, light-hearted to serious and political.

As always Maitra writes with passion and the poems vibrate with his heart-beats.

Contents

Going to England

He and his brother Raj
wait eagerly for Saraswati Puja:
She would bless their schoolbooks.
They make chains of coloured papers –
red, blue and green.
Dad had bought them from
Kolkata's New Market.
Standing on stools
the boys hang them high
criss-crossing to form a roof.
Dad and uncle Ravi lift
the Goddess up and place her
under the decorative loops.
He gazes at Saraswati. She fixes him
with her painted wide eyes.
Her red lips, slightly parted,
move as if for a second.
He hears a voice, and then it's gone.
Soon they're told to go to bed.
In the dark, Raj whispers,
'Which books did you leave
below her feet? I like her blessings
on my Math.' 'English. She told me
I'm going to England one day.'

A seed's planted

The doctor is coming.
Soon everything will be fine.
He remembers the hush
that wrapped their first floor flat.

The man arrives, tall grey-haired
in pristine white, gets to work
gently probing his brother's abdomen
in unhurried silence, writes a prescription
and leaves. The patient's tummy pain
vanishes with the medicine as if by magic.
He vows that day he'd be a Medic.
Later, as a doctor, he saw the magic
of a surgeon's sharp knife.

The journey

The voices of his mum and dad
and almost the entire neighbourhood
still ring in his ears as he stands
in front of the desk: a white face arms
two blue eyes that shoot at him,
a glance, soon a dark stare, then it shifts
like a searchlight onto his documents,
passport. A dryness coils out of his chest
and reaches the throat tightening it slowly,
a thick snake. 'What's the purpose of your visit,
Doctor?' He tries to recall the descriptive speech
he's rehearsed at length with his hospital friends.
In stead he blurts out: 'I want to be a surgeon,
a Fellow of the Royal College, London, England.'
The officer stamps hurriedly on the page
as if overwhelmed. He collects his gold
and speeds through the passage, his sweat
now a downpour. A cousin meets him
as he comes out carrying a large suitcase
full of books. A gust of cold air blows
as he walks towards the Underground,
a large sign reads, 'Welcome to England.'

First snowfall

Snow fell all night. This morning
it's all white. He looks out
of the postage stamp window –
flecks still coming down.
He shivers, in the corner
the small gas-fire flickers. Later
he'd go out and taste the first
winter in England: feet crunching
the ice and cold wind numbing
his face. Before that he must
tidy his small sagging bed,
the landlady's very strict, and
look in last week's BMJ for any job.
The door slowly opens, he lifts
his eyes from the page and looks
straight into a large Alsatian,
inches away. The dog's breath
wafts into his nose, he freezes.
Minutes seem hours, his throat dries.
He'd seen the animal before,
the owner's guard and pet.
As he ponders the next step
the beast barks once and leaves.
He shuts the door tight,
and decides to savour the splendour
of his first snowfall locked inside.

The lucky day

He stands, still out of breath, in front of
The Infirmary, a small redbrick building.
The front door's shut, he looks at his watch,
and rings the bell. A face pops up and asks, 'Yes?'
'I've come for the interview.' He gives
his name. 'You're late! Very late. But it's
your lucky day. They're still in the office.'
He's ushered into a carpeted room.
Two men sit at one end of a long table.
One, bald, in green theatre clothes
and a white coat, twiddles his glasses and
wipes the lenses again and again. The other,
in suit and tie, shakes his hands.
'I'm Peter Jenkins, the hospital secretary,
and this is Dr. Roger Small,
Senior Consultant Anaesthetist.'
He mumbles, 'Hello,' and tastes his dry throat.
'Sorry I'm delayed. The train...'
'Not to worry, you're here. We'll just ask you
a few questions and it'd be soon over.'
Later he catches the Glasgow Express.
In a couple of hours he'd be at the flat
he shares with jobless foreign graduates.
Slowly a voice rises inside his head,
'You want to be a surgeon, not an anaesthetist,
not the side show but the main act!'
Through the window he watches the green
landscape whizzes past. This post a mistake,
perhaps. But no, at last he's got a job,
a stepping-stone, he'd now plan his route.
Later he learnt he's the only candidate
and they're desperate to appoint someone.

Baptism of fire (1)

'Doctor, I want you to start this case,'
the man with the spectacles says.
'Yes Dr. Small, sir,' a tremor
shakes his voice. The anaesthetic nurse
ties a rubber band round the patient's arm,
and hands him a loaded syringe –
Pentothal, the induction drug.
He taps the front of the elbow,
feels, and then plunges the needle
into the skin pulling on the piston
to see whether he's inside the vein.
But no blood comes out; he withdraws
and strikes again at a different site.
Slowly the whole area a black and blue map.
'Stop that, doctor, you're hurting
Mrs Jones.' Consultant snatches away
the lethal weapon from his hands.
'Stay away, and don't touch her again.'
He stands in the corner, a leper.
'Didn't they teach you the basics?
You've to start from scratch.'
He couldn't explain he'd been looking
for work for months, just rusty, that's all.
This isn't the job he wanted. But
the consultant's words strike him
like bullets. He vows he'll be the best
anaesthetic SHO the Infirmary ever had.

A teaching session

'Doctor, bring a stool and sit
beside me,' Poly Perkins says.
She likes the SHO to be with her
when she gives anaesthetics.
'I'll teach you to be really good.'
He listens intently how to muster
the basics and the latest techniques.
Her words soothing like that of a friend,
not of a junior consultant.
That day as she talks he can feel
her breath on his face – a hint
of a perfume he hasn't noticed
before, and a fluttering of her eyelashes.
At one stage she says softly,
'You must miss your home cooking.
Why don't I do a meal for you this weekend?
It'd be a change from the hospital cold meat.'
'Thanks very much. You're so kind.'
Her detached house in the outskirts
of the town a picture: neat lawns, flowers,
thick carpets, paintings on the walls,
souvenirs from India and Far East:
'I love your house.' 'Take a seat.
Have a drink. You drink, don't you?'
He nods, but has only tasted alcohol
once before. Whiskey burns his throat.
She's cooked roast lamb, vegetables
and Basmati rice. They drank wine.
'I'll call a taxi to take you back.
Don't worry, just relax.' They sit on a sofa.
Her face comes closer. His heart
kicks him in the ribs. Then she
suddenly withdraws. 'Oh my god,
look at the time. I'll ring for a cab.'
Later lying on his bed in the doctors'
quarter he asks himself – is she a teacher,
lover or a friend? Only silence echoes
in the darkness.

A surgeon appreciates

'Hi doc, how are you today?'
Mr. Wilkins, the Canadian surgeon, booms.
'I see you've got Mrs. Roberts ready.
Keep her really relaxed, son.
When I get into her belly I want
the muscles to be soft like jelly
so that I can hunt down the little stones
in the duct after taking out the nasty sac.'
'Yes sir, you'll find everything just perfect.'
He likes this master craftsman
whose blade an artist's brush.
In no time abdomen opened,
gall bladder found and removed –
'Sister, send this please to the Lab.'
His large confidant hands search
for the elusive bits hiding in the bile
duct, and one by one take them out.
'Thank you all.' Then to the anaesthetist,
'Great job again, my young friend.'
The big man retires and waits
for the next case. In the recovery room
the young apprentice slowly wakes up
the patient, and dreams some day
he'd be that giant with a delicate touch.

Where did it go wrong?

'Doctor, please come to the ward,
Mr. Johnson has collapsed.'
'You mean Paul Johnson
who just had his hernia repaired?'
'Yes doctor. He's fine after he came back,
then started to cough and passed out.'
He runs with the nurse along the corridor,
seconds last minutes, his pulse races
like a racehorse being whipped.
The seventy-year old lies motionless
on the bed, a nurse holds a mask over the face
and squeezes oxygen into the lungs.
He bends down and feels the pulse –
'thready' and fast, the breathing shallow
and slow. 'I've to intubate; call Dr. Perkins
and the Team.' They work like in a scene
from Casualty but the heart won't start.
The consultant takes him to a side and says,
'It's not your fault he died. You did
everything by the book. This would be
a Coroner's case but I bet you won't be blamed.'
At the inquest no cause of death found.
'Sometimes patients die in spite of
everything we do. And it happens
to all of us. It's hard the first time,
almost like losing a close friend.
But you would survive.'
Days pass. Time blankets the memory
but once in a while that face appears
and whispers, 'You put me to sleep.
It's your duty to wake me up.'

The first test (Primary FRCS)

'Come in, come in, treat it as your
own home. We'd Indian doctors
with us before. They're so happy.'
The old lady shows him the room,
small but tidy and warm. He's booked
this B&B in Dublin for the exam,
he must pass it, the first part, and then
the Final to win the glittering prize, FRCS,
dream letters a surgeon must have
after his name. On the day of the test
he's up at dawn, snatches a toast,
half-drinks a cup and reaches the big hall
crowded with aspiring young surgeons.
Next few hours pass in a trance –
writing down answers, pausing,
trying to remember the structures
of bones, joints, muscles, nerves,
and how the organs like Pancreas work,
and finally face the examiners discussing
specimens of cut out body parts in jars.
The landlady asks, 'How did it go?'
'Alright,' but inside an uncertainty nags.
'I know you'd pass,' the landlady says.
And he did. 'You deserve a treat.'
That evening she cooks Irish stew.
For the first time in days he feels
he could eat a whole plate.
Under the gentle ceiling light, the knife
in his hand glints as he cuts the meat.

Christmas dinner

'You sit beside me, I'll look after you,'
says the smiling sister Shaw,
a large woman whose words are law
on the surgical ward. But she was the first
to say 'Hello' when he came to work
as the new SHO, and extend her hand.
She also said, 'Doctor, these are the rules;
follow them please and we'll be fine.'
He'd done that: come at 7, examined
his patients, written down histories,
taken blood and sent them for tests
long before Mr. Wilkins started round.
'How is he doing, sister?' the booming
voice of the Canadian echoes round the walls.
'Fine, sir, I've shown him the ropes,
and he's working hard.'
'Good. Now, you must think like a surgeon
and not a gasman. And it isn't easy –
anaesthesia and surgery seem like twins
but...' he winks. The young medic
wants to tell him he's always been
a surgeon, anaesthesia just a stepping-stone.
'Are you dreaming again, doctor,
food is getting cold,' Sister Shaw
gives him a nudge. 'Sorry.' He starts
shoving turkey and Brussels sprout
into his mouth. Later she pulls him
onto the floor. 'Sister I can't dance,'
he groans. 'Rubbish,' she grabs him
and begins to swing her hips.
He clings to her and prays, 'Please god,
let this nightmare end before too long.'

A party

'We're having a party. You must come.'
He hesitates. 'Jill's depending on you.
She's your number one fan.'
He remembers the second year nurse –
always a smile on her face.
'I'll be there.' Most bring cans of beer,
coke, and someone a bottle of gin.
They sit in the Residents' lounge,
doctors and nurses drinking and
chatting. Someone dims the light.
Pairs kiss, cuddle and hug.
'Are you enjoying your training?'
he asks Jill. 'Yes. I like working
on the surgical ward best. But
soon I'd be posted to the Geriatrics.
There the doctors not like you,
and the old people so demanding!'
Then she whispers, 'Please don't
tell sister. She'd be mad.' 'I won't.'
He doesn't know what to say next.
Suddenly asks, innocent as a boy,
'What shall we do now?'
'Don't you know? Look around.'
Her face comes closer to his,
her perfume jumps out from her skin.
He tries to open his lips
but can't as if sealed by glue.
He moves away to breathe.
She gives him a piercing look,
and leaves. He lingers for a minute
and returns to his cold bed.
He can't understand why but
something's holding him back –
as if like a soldier he needs to focus
on his task, and has no time to relax?
He clenches his fist till it hurts.

Misread signals

'Doctor, do you like a cuppa? I'm
making one for myself.' Amanda,
a third year nurse on night shift, says.
He's gone to the ward to check on
his patients and have a chat.
'Yes please, I love one.'
He watches her move, her pink uniform
wraps her like a pet snake. He sighs.
'Have you heard from home?'
'Yes, got a telegram from dad.'
'What did he say?' 'Well done son,
passing your exam at the first try.'
His brown eyes light up.
'When would you celebrate?'
'Who with?' 'I'll come and have a drink.'
'What about this meal-break?'
'You mean tonight?
Naughty boy!' Her face lights up.
Later in his bedroom he hears
her knock and ushers her in.
They drink coke and tonic.
Days later he meets her again.
'Would you like to go for a curry?
You told me you liked spicy food.'
'I'm sorry. Really, really sorry.
My boyfriend John a very jealous man.
I'm sure you'd find someone soon
and prettier than me. Good luck.'
Suddenly his world turns black.

Varicose veins

'You do the ankle, I'll do the groin,'
Mr Cohen, the consultant, says.
He's been waiting for those words
for weeks. 'Yes sir. Thank you, sir.'
He'd assisted the surgeon many times
during the past months. At last
his luck's turned. He starts dissecting
the long Saphenous vein at the lower end
carefully preserving the nerve
and then waits for the surgeon
to finish his part, and pass the metal
stripper down so that the vein
could be pulled out from the groin.
'Sister, packs, more packs. I think
one of the ligatures has slipped.'
He can see his consultant's sweaty forehead.
Minutes pass. 'Shall I call Mr. Brewster?'
Sister asks. 'But he's on leave.'
'Sorry, someone must take over now.
I'm not ...' Mr. Cohen collapses
on the floor. 'Call the Team!'
the gasman shouts, and turning to him,
'Yes doctor, you must finish the job.'
He moves to the upper end,
a buzz in his head, and the lights glare
as if he's entered an unreal world.
Later they all shake his hand.
'Well done. Well done. Doctor.'
Sitting in the residents' lounge
he relives the scene again and again
to be sure it wasn't all a dream.

A registrar

In the small waiting room they stare
at the wall trying to avoid each other's
eyes. One plays with her handbag, others
bite nails or rearrange their ties.
He's seen the opposition: two English –
a man and a woman, and two Indians –
both men. He's spoken to his countryman –
Satiprasad Kar from Wrexham, FRCS.
'I'm from Liverpool,' he'd said timidly
and admitted he'd be taking the Final
next month. 'FRCS, you're sure to get a job.'
But Kar had whispered, 'Look at the locals,
we've no chance.' The interview starts:
Kar first and he's last, he picks up
a magazine and tries to read.
Finally his name's called. The selectors
sit like judges in a court; the chairman says
'I see Mr. Cohen thinks highly of you.'
The ice breaks, he breathes easily and answers
questions about work, what he wants to be,
like having a conversation. But when finished
he notes his vest dripping with sweat.
Who would be the lucky ones, who'd go back
empty-handed? Suddenly the door
opens, and the clerk calls Mr Kar's name.
And then he hears his. His heart leaps.
He goes inside to shake hands. 'Give my regards
to Jack Cohen and keep up the good work,'
the surgeon pats him on the back. Outside
the hospital gate Mr Sati Kar says,
'I was wrong, merit counts. Congratulations.'
'And you too.' He heads home knowing
a new road has opened up, but it'd be tough.

Baptism of fire (2)

He scrubs up, and ready to go. Theatre lights
dazzle his eyes in the middle of the night.
An emergency – a woman with appendicitis,
he's the registrar on call, FRCS after his name,
a 'bread and butter' task, no need to alert
the consultant or Mr. James, the other experienced
registrar, 'Scalpel please, staff-nurse.'
He cuts the skin, blood spills and spurts,
nurse swabs. He stops the bleeding and
begins to wade through layers and layers of fat.
At last he's inside, and picks up loops of bowel,
balls of fat glide over his gloves.
He searches for the culprit but it plays
Hide & Seek. Sweat, pearls, collect
on his forehead. Wall clock tick-tocks,
anaesthetist hovers, nurses exchange glances.
Where's the bastard organ? His face burns.
'Can you please retract a bit harder?
Will anyone please re-adjust the light?'
He frets. 'Do you think we ought to send for
Mr. James?' No. No. Then everyone would
know how weakling's the new registrar.
But they call the Australian, twice his age.
He assists as Mr. James finishes the op,
and later in the changing room puts a hand
on his shoulder and says, 'It's a difficult case,
she's so fat.' But he knows now, 'A surgeon
doesn't give up when the going gets tough.'

The special place

Everyone waits. It's his first planned operating list.
He enters like an actor on stage. A buzz fills his head,
his eyes shine with the bright light, assistants and nurses
talk in low voices – the hum drums up his heartbeat.
He feels in his bone this is his special place.

He scrubs, the brush rubs his nails and palms.
Lather rolls slowly off his skin, reluctant to leave,
the green gown petal soft, gloves hug his hands,
a lover's kiss. But he knows these are forerunners
of the main act that will soon start.

'Scalpel, scissors, ligatures' – words shoot out of his mouth,
rapid-fire missiles. He sweats under his mask, mutters
to himself and works patiently on his anatomical canvas,
a battle-hungry soldier-artist. Stitches print his signature
as he ends the case, then changes ready to begin the next.

A sleepless night

'You won't sleep tonight,' the surgeon says.
Simple words but they punch a hole
in his chest. He's just told the boss
what went wrong with his op – he's securing
the vessel and taking the gall bladder out
when the ligature slipped, it bled and bled
deep inside. He'd put packs after packs
and prayed. Bleeding did stop but he couldn't
find the artery's cut end. He left a drain
and closed up the incision.
'You'd stay awake, stare at your phone
and wait. Any moment it might ring
and you'd shoot out of your bed, you know
your patient's life is at stake.'
He wants to disappear into a hole.
'You could have asked for help.
But you didn't. So stew in your juice.'
That night his patient's pale face
haunts him every time his eyelids close.
'Thank you, doctor,' Mrs. Molloy
shakes his hands in the ward next day.
'You've done a splendid job.'
But he knows he'd taken a chance,
and a surgeon should never bank on luck.

How long have I got?

Sitting in the surgeon's room he recollects
the words of his last patient: a thirty-two-year old
mum with a lump in her breast, after he told her
the diagnosis, 'How long have I got? Doctor,
how long? I want the truth.' Her eyes blazed.
'I know tomorrow I'm your first case.' She takes
a breath, 'Please tell me. I must know.' Her voice
thick as suffocating smoke. 'Mrs Campbell,
you've every chance of doing well. And then
Mr. Smith, the plastic surgeon, would
reconstruct your breast. He's excellent!'
But she wasn't listening any more, her gaze
wandered, as if she didn't really want to know.
Next day she lies in bed, a large dressing on her chest
and a plastic drain. Husband sits holding her hand.
Nurses come regularly and check. Monitors bleep, bleep.
He completes his round, and goes to the clinic.
But his pace slows momentarily as he hears
her voice follow him, 'Doc, how long have I got?'

The journey's end

'Sorry. You're good, but competition's
stiff for Senior Registrars' posts.'
The selectors' words echo in his brain
as he leaves the interview room. He knows
without a senior registrar's training
he'd never be a NHS consultant.
And the reason clear, but he wants to hear it
from his boss. Next day the consultant
and his registrar operate on their patients
in adjoining theatres. 'Good morning, sir.'
'Morning, how did it go?' He shakes his head.
'Sorry to hear that.' Later during a break
he asks, looking straight at his boss's face,
'Sir what're my chances?' 'You mean
to be in time a consultant surgeon?'
'Yes.' 'It's a difficult question.'
Mr. Collins looks at the ceiling while getting
changed, then turns to his registrar and says,
'You want the truth?' 'I do.'
'I rate you a top grade surgeon, but
the perception is the public isn't ready
for a coloured consultant.
It'll happen but I don't know when.'
Later in adjoining theatres two surgeons,
the consultant and his register, finish
their near identical lists. But for him
the journey has finally come to an end.

The final goodbye

On the last day walls
close in from all sides.
The overhead lamp
dulls, a haze. He moves
slowly stretching out
his seconds, chats, but
his throat dries up
as he finishes his list.
Everyone wishes
him good luck.
'You've been a great team,'
he replies, but can't
utter the words,
'I'll miss you and this
place very much;'
the professional has
put on his mask and
tucked away the tears
of the final goodbye.

Another casualty

She lies on a trolley, a rag doll,
her brown face pale under the light
of the Resuscitation Room.
The right arm blown off from the wrist;
doctors and nurses move quickly,
give blood, connect her to machines
that bleep-bleep; a flicker on her
wounded face and lips – 'She's coming
round! BP low! Heart rate rapid!'
Surgeons concentrate to save
her arm and assess other injuries.
'Where does it hurt'? doctors ask.
'Sorry mum,' she whispers, like
a secret prayer and closes her eyes.
She does not recognise the young woman
who 'Blew herself up at an empty
bus stop. No other casualties.'

After days in the Intensive Care Unit,
she touches her tender scars, straightens
her arm and leg – the pain from electric
shocks! What was she trying to achieve?
Protesting at the world's madness or seeking
revenge for her brother? She could still
hear him chatter about going to college,
then abroad, being an engineer or a medic
only to be crushed under the rubble of their
house when helicopter gun-ships fired rockets
in Gaza city. Tears roll down her cheeks
as the amputated arm shakes.

Trapped

She enters my consulting room
and buzzes the space round her. Later
her perfume spreads like a net
as she settles on the satin-covered chair.

A split black silk skirt struggles
to wrap her legs when she crosses them
in slow motion. She watches me
stealing a glance as she confirms her name.

Head still she begins her history.
I focus on the rhythmically moving lips
as if locked in, hear her voice caress
the air and wave into me. She grips

the table. 'It was a terrible crash,
he ruined my life' – her blue eyes
shoot laser beams. She takes deep breaths
pressing her breasts against the blouse.

Soon her tale ends. I complete
my examination and shake her hand.
She shakes her head tossing her hair.
It floats like embracing wings. She stands

at the door for a minute teasing the knob
and then leaves. Her aroma still wraps
round the room. I stare at the chair
where she sat.   Trapped.

The red bricks talk

Bulldozers smash the walls breaking the bricks.
Large trucks, slow ambulances, pick up
and dispose the remains. No flashing light.
Soon a mega glass/aluminium beast rises
from the heart of the old Casualty where patients,
friends and relatives queued, had a chat
with the nurse, a cup of tea for the bereaved,
a few drunks slobbered and swore, and one or two
'regulars' who had nowhere to go.

In the new-look A & E receptionists, nurses
in bright coloured tunic, triage and register
patients on touch-sensitive computer screens –
electronic boards display waiting times in red,
'Doctor,' 'Nurse,' 'Surgeon,' 'Anaesthetist' fleet in
and out, overhead signs direct to McDonald and KFC,
X-ray, Lab. Waiting area packed, but only a hum,
no loud voices except for a drunk soon removed.

Some days 'old-timers' and 'regulars' still come,
chat about bygone days, and claim to hear
the red bricks talk – how lives were saved and lost,
of bleary eyes and tired hands; of eating birthday cakes,
and giving 'blanket-baths' to those leaving, and how
doctors or nurses had time to talk. They cock
their ears to hear the stories they already know
to remember a dear departed friend.

Numbers

999 calls brought in three *Cardiac Arrests.*
Their ages: Sixty, Fifty-five and Twenty-five.
I've to ring the GPs about the deaths.

The first doctor I ring isn't surprised.
He was half-expecting the news.
The 60-year-old had Angina, heart-bypass,
just marking time. The second patient,
55, was on the mend. Her fractured leg
was just out of cast. Why did she die?
'Must be a dislodged blood clot –
Pulmonary Embolism,' we speculate.

I pause before making the third call,
The 30-year-old 'Found hanged.'
Paramedics thumped and shocked
him at home, we too worked hard but
his heart refused to start, the engine
of a burnt-out car. He's on Prozac,
and supposed to be doing well.
I kept seeing the circling grey mark,
a coiled snake round his neck.

Driving back home I accelerate, watch
car's speedometer needle swing and touch
'twenty-five, fifty-five, sixty,' sending a shiver
down my spine.

My Gladstone bag

They gave me the bag – shiny
dark, red Italian leather with a brass lock.
'You could put all your hand luggage
in it and travel the whole world.'
I felt its inviting soft touch,
smelled the skin, fresh as if alive
waiting for me to take the plunge.
But when I opened and looked
the empty space stared back
like the inside of an eviscerated corpse:
where are the syringe, bandage,
scalpel, pills and gloves?
Do they want me to forget
what I was, and what I always will be?
'Anyone can be a traveller
after they shake your hand and say goodbye.'
I hear a voice proclaim in my head,
'You are not finished yet,
let that bag stay empty,
it's not a travelling kit.'

Don't want to be late

Don't want to be late. So I go to my clinic
hotfooted. Receptionist's eyes widen.
She simply says, Room 10. I see no one waits.

I open my door: windows curtained off
as if hiding a secret, cream-coloured walls
warm under a strip-light. I put down my bundle
of notes on the desk and ease into the chair.

I read the day's list: Jones, McBride, Smith,
and picture how they'd come, sit,
hold their hands on the lap, look round, speak,
disperse their body-smells – vinegar-sweat
or showered freshness that'd vibrate in the air,
hear their different voices and stories.
Then notice I'm an hour early, and think
may be the clinic would finish early too.

The phone rings. My first patient's in.
A knock on the door. 'Hello Mrs Jones,
come in and take a seat.' 'Doctor, I am a Miss,'
thunders a large woman crashing on
the chair opposite. Gently I shake her hand
and feel in my bones, today I'd be very late.

My muscles

A four-year-old, blue-eyed like his dad.
He's strapped in the back on a trip
to the seaside – a treat; dad had come
home, a brief leave from the front.
Another car went into the back of theirs.
A sore neck for a few days, then he's fine.
I examine dad first, a tattooed muscled
young man, and declare him fully recovered.
'Can I see you now?' I ask the little boy.
He gets up, walks towards me and stands
still like a trooper, looking straight
into my eyes, no dropping of eyelids
or staring down at his feet. 'He's not shy,'
dad said smiling. I asked him to move
his neck this way and that. He did all, an old hat.
Before he left he pointed to his arm
and whispered, 'My muscles!'

An extra patient

A blond one-year-old crawls on the floor,
sometimes looking up at me smiling.
'Sorry, my wife's working, I'd to bring her.'
'No problem,' I carry on and examine
his burns scars from a burst hot water pipe.
She gives a cursory glance once, then
carries on playing: grabbing at absent objects
in her secret world, talking to them in words
that are just sounds, a drop of saliva hangs
from her lips, she keeps moving, sliding on her
bottom and then up on to her knees and reaches
the door as my examination ends. 'Time to go,'
dad says, picks up and kisses his daughter.
'Say bye, bye to the doctor.' 'Bye, bye,'
we say to each other, she waves her hands –
my extra patient who came only to play.

Mind game

I sit in the clinic obscurely among many –
in fact no one is looking at me. I'm a patient
like them – but the white coat betrays me.
I sense their laser eyes dissecting the layers
of my past: what sort of boy I was in school,
a timid soul who did the teachers' bidding,
cramming page after page and pass exams?

What sort of doctor I am? Did I struggle
through years of Medical School – faint
in the Anatomy room or collapse at the
first sight of blood? How did I deal with
the mother of a kid lying badly injured or
the wife of a man dying from Cardiac Arrest?
How many mistakes have I made? Do I
suffer from my ills like the others, but know
how the system works and will bypass everyone?

Then nurse calls the next one on the list.
I shuffle in my seat. No one looks at me.
I'm a patient waiting my turn like the rest.

The skeleton in my cupboard

wasn't a secret. I bought it to study Anatomy.
I'd take it out at weekends, and sometime
during nights. Hanging from a thick pole
its empty orbits watched me as I mastered
the structure of the skull, the spine – joined up
vertebrae that looked like short-wing pork pies,
pelvis, arms and legs, long and short bones
and the clever architecture of the shoulder and hip.
Slowly I grew fond of this man. What's he like
when he's alive? A miner who toiled under
the earth? A factory worker on gruelling shifts?
Or someone well off who donated his body
to the science?
No, he's a gravedigger, he told me as he rattled
his bones coming out of the cupboard, and
waking me up, how he buried bodies dressed
in Sunday best. 'People are peaceful when dead,
the rich and the poor – all skeletons in the end.'
'Who were you talking to last night?' mum asked.
'No one. I was practising for the exam.' I heard
him many more times in my sleep after that.
Now I've no skeleton in my cupboard but
a secret we shared.

Shred

'Make sure you don't shred things
you want to keep,' a retired friend
told me once. In my office I stare
at the empty sacs, marked 'CONFIDENTIAL,
SHRED,' and then the bulging shelves.
I open a box file marked 'Private' and
turn the pages, a shade yellow, and
smell of vinegar. Names – Johnson, Russell,
Jones, Sen, many blurred faces. Read
the references I wrote in confidence.
'Was I fair?' I wish I could tell them now.
I put back the documents. Another box.
Papers published, papers rejected.
I skip, then pick up at random: duty rotas,
seminars, Disaster Plans, NHS Directives.
They are for the skip. I breathe a little easy.
Then I find more boxes, my progress slows.
'SHRED, SHRED,' the sacs shout but
the list of *things* I intend to keep steadily grows.

Poverty

It is easy to talk about poverty
when you see a black child on the Box
holding a small bowl, half-filled
with maize-paste, licking his fingers,
flies buzzing round his dust-smeared face,
behind him the endless desert hissing.

It is easy to talk about poverty
when a woman in a torn sari begs
in a bustling urban street,
one hand outstretched and half-cupped
and the other clutching an infant,
small and limp, to her breast.

It is easy to talk about poverty
when Blair-Bush – the G8 kings –
gather at Glen Eagle, their freedom
of speech unchecked inside steel fences,
dining with best salmon and vintage
Boudeaux, far from the hemmed-in
crowd that wants to talk about truth.

But is it fair to talk about poverty
and splatter the globe with words
while another hungry child dies?

A Bangladeshi corner shopkeeper

(According to Denise Levertov)

When did you leave Bangladesh?
In the Sixties when the Beatles came.
Did you like music? Did you sing in Bangladesh?
We sang as our boat rode river Ganges,
'Hilsha, Hilsha, you silver mirror fish,
the Harvest of Ganges – our fertile mother.'
That sounds good, a perfect life?
Then came the monsoon and the flood,
angry Ganges burst its banks,
Hilshas floated gasping for breath.
Our Hilsha would not swim again.
Did the Government offer help?
They built a dam that trapped
our river, it became a cowed canal.
Now, in Britain what do you do?
Sell chilies and mints, papers and biscuits.
I exist.
Are the locals friendly? Do they smile?
'Morning' they say, then pay and leave
with their magazines and cigarettes.
Do you smile? Do you still sing? Hum?
Dream of going back and not return?
I'm here for good – just a corner shopkeeper,
but every night when I go to bed I smile
and sing in my head, Hilsha, Hilsha,
you silver mirror fish, you swim in my mind,
you've crossed the open seas, and fulfilled my wish.

The Pyramid-seller of Cairo

A young Arab appears in front of me
blocking my view of the Great Pyramid.
He wears a white shirt and a pair of jeans.
'Where are you from?' he asks, tone friendly,
his eyes soft on my brown skin. I see trinkets
and T-shirts on his arms.

'England,' I reply. 'I have an uncle in London,'
he says. 'You can visit him, then?' He shakes
his head. 'I've a family: see, my daughter, my son,
nine and seven.' He shows and points at the photos.
I notice her rush of black hair, his toothy smile.
'Very nice,' I respond and move to re-join our group.
'Please, I want to give you this,' he pushes
a plastic-wrapped garment towards my hand.
I refuse and leave. His eyes darken and follow me.

Sitting in the coach I think of the man's kids:
would he tell them that he met someone
of his own colour from England? Would he
stay awake dreaming of Big Ben? That one day
he would, like me, see it in flesh? Would he
feel betrayed that I didn't buy; I didn't help?

We pick up speed. The sun beats down on
the Great Pyramid and the people at its feet.
The stone-monument now distant and small,
almost a picture-postcard, the Pyramid-seller
expands in my mind; true or false he gnawed
inside my head with the sharp teeth of guilt.

'Collateral damage'

The civilian casualties, the collateral damage –
the price must be paid, our leaders say,
to win the war against terror.
We read it in the papers, and watch on TV:

a boy crouches with his dad pinned
against a pock-marked wall of a shantytown
in Gaza Strip clutching his father's vest.
Shots ring round, his fingers slacken,
then slither down to the ground.
Army sharpshooters reload and aim.

A man staggers from pouring dust cloud
that swirls and wraps New York's sky-scrappers.
He wipes blood from his blackened forehead,
and struggles for breath in Paramedic's arms.
On her mobile a woman whispers, 'I love you.'

From the sky planes drop laser-guided bombs
that burst open the mountains and scatter
Afghanistan's dust. In the villages children play,
and pick up chocolates that rain from heavens
parcelled in yellow shells guaranteed not to explode,
too innocent to understand the danger they face.

'Collateral damage' 'Collateral damage' –
politicians explain while we watch the killing fields
fill up with the dead.

Doing business with the enemy

The small marina outside the town buzzes
with busloads of holiday-makers, many
like us have chosen to come to Cuba
to experience how one man defied the superpower
and lived to tell the tale. In the restaurant
chicken, beef, paste, cheese, Spanish beer
and local rum on the menu as if it's just another
Caribbean island. Also a private harbour with
a few luxury sailing boats moored.
We eat, drink and chat – the usual holiday gossip.
Soon we prepare to leave in our air-conditioned
coaches to continue our tour. The waitresses
and men in the bar begin clearing up for
next day and another batch of tourists.
On the road outside a man rides a horse-taxi
up and down looking in vain for customers.
Crowds gather at bus stop and wait hours.
I picture the men and women who served us
going to their tiny home or flat, savouring
a meal of rice and beans. As the place fades
in the distance, the two pictures – the natives
and the tourists – collide inside my head. I ask,
'Dear Cuba, have you given up your fight
to uphold, "each according to his need
and not greed," because to feed your people
you have to do business with the enemy?'

The rebellion of the shoes

Sitting on a bench at the city centre
shopping arcade, my bored eyes drift
to a window-display of shoes: brown, black
yellow and white. They glint in the light,
some with the latest designer labels,
and point to the left, the right, in clusters
and rows beside a 'Sale' sign.

A group of them look straight at me
as if urging me to press a switch which,
in a trance, I do instinctively in my mind
and watch, like in a video game, the shoes
burst through the glass, march along
the corridor tapping the soles, laughter
in their steps. The shoppers, passers-by
converse, fuss about prices, ignorant of
the jailbreak, that the shoes would
no longer be their slaves, to be trodden
on by feet. They want a new life.

Then I wake up and begin to walk home
crushing the shoes' fantasy dream.

Modern-day slaves

Young black men sell handbags and sunglasses
in the streets of Florence – fake designer goods
on makeshift stalls, blankets on tarmac, each
the size of a large tablecloth. They fold up and
hide when police cars make the rounds and then
return to their spots as the 'law' moves to the next job.
A few passers-by stop and look at the goods.
The men entice them in broken English, Italian or French:
'Madam! Sir! Just feel the leather! Try the glasses!
It's a real bargain!' No one buys.
They watch the diners in the pavement restaurants
eating pizza, pasta, spaghetti. The spicy, cheesy smell
churns their empty stomachs spinning their brains
with the memories of freshly-cooked cobs of maize
in the shantytowns of Ghana, Uganda or Botswana.
The slavery's abolished; no one is sold in open markets.
But didn't I see them on the streets of Florence,
the modern-day slaves
                              trying to break the chain?

A woollen cardigan

For my birthday you buy a cardigan. The label
doesn't say where it was made. Perhaps Pakistan,
India, Thailand or Singapore by brown or
yellow-skinned hands toiling under a few fans

to fashion exotic patterns of radiant colours,
blue, white and red interlaced, playful snakes.
I could almost smell the spicy dusty air, and
feel the sweltering heat of the confined space

in the factories where rows of women work
bent over old machines, see the fear in their eyes
of not finishing quotas, losing jobs, hear
their whispered foreign tongue and sighs.

'They do make wonderful things,' you enthuse.
'And so cheap!' In the office a colleague says,
'Your wife has good taste.' You want to know
whether they liked it or not. I mumble, 'Yes.'

But don't you know when I wear the cardigan
to please you, those embroidered snakes
suddenly come alive, and I can't breathe
as the creatures tighten round my chest?

By the third shroud I

have stopped counting.
Death of one, an accident,
illness or homicide, limited
in its scale even if the grief's
heart-rending to the bereaved.
A burial is arranged
and then, in a way, it's ended.
Two, a little more taxing –
but no more than that.
When I come to the third
I think of a mass grave
where the identity of one
lost by the fatality of many,
instinctively I search my soul:
I know I wasn't a guard
at a concentration camp,
or took part in Pol Pot's Killing Fields
or dropped bombs on Gaza Strip.
But I feel complicit in all of these,
I'm part of the same human race.

Burnt-out seconds

Coming back home from posting
a few poems to beat the deadline
I spot the dirty window ledge.
Taking a bowl of water I mix it
with washing-up soap and clean
sloshing liquid froth all over the PVC.
I strike up a rhythm with my hands
moving to and fro – a rhythm I can't
manage on my keyboard trying
to spin imageries in fictions and poems.
Then I inspect the result and find
stubborn black dots stare at me, defying
the extra effort I'd put in. I could do
it again and wipe them out for good
but not from my poems where they persist
in the stalled start, the wandering middle
and the hesitant last lines – my burnt-out seconds.

Thakurdah

The old man I never really knew
looks down from the picture on the wall.
His delicate cheek bones and thin lips
belie his age and wrinkles of time.

My grandfather was an ordinary clerk
in a large office filled with files.
His pen climbed every day
up Himalayas of paperwork.

The pen in my hand carefully writes
the history of patients and their operations.
My fingers pick up scalpel and forceps
to routinely complete a mundane task.

The old man I thought I never knew
looks down from the picture on the wall.
My scalpel rests. I have picked up a pen
and mountains of files are full of my poems.

A lost and found game

'Let's go for a picnic at the Botanical Garden
to celebrate your home visit,' my uncle said.
'You can also see The Great Tree again.'
Last time I went there granddad was with us,
I got lost and he found me. He told us stories about
The Great Banyan Tree, and that spirits of the dead
lived under its shade, one could communicate
with them if one had faith.
At the Garden on a patch of green we set up
a makeshift oven, and women began to cook.
Soon the smell of ginger, turmeric, and chilli
spiced up my tongue. 'I'll go for a walk, won't get lost.'
I reached a forest of thick branches and roots
arising from one trunk, a Himalayan umbrella;
underneath it's cool, I felt a shiver. There's a musty
earthy smell that filled my lungs, I sensed
I'd hear him or feel his touch any moment
but only the tourists' chat and clicking cameras
broke the silence.
Later eating rice with spinach and aubergine,
we talked about a cousin's job promotion,
and the impending wedding of someone else.
But I couldn't concentrate, my mind kept
returning to that Tree playing a Lost and Found game.

You may find yourself

in Newcastle on your break from work,
strolling along city centre streets, looking at
the lunchtime crowd munching sandwiches,
window-shopping; pubs, restaurants displaying
special offer menus in white chalk on pavement
black-boards, a couple smoking and eating chips
outside the Housing Benefit Office, and a young man
begging outside the Cathedral's closed doors.

Or you may find yourself

on a holiday in Kolkata, your home, taking
a morning walk picking your way between bodies
lying on paving stones like corpses except they move,
cough, inhaling the oil/egg smell from a black pan
frying the first breakfast omelette on the street; mega-kettles
blowing steam-snakes, terracotta cups lined for a fill,
the beggar starting the day with a rag and a bowl,
and a dog searching in a rubbish heap.

Or you may find yourself

in another country and a different street.
But where ever you are, you'd wish you're
somewhere else, your search ended,
and your hunger a thing of the past.

The diary

In a drawer I find an old diary, 1961,
the year I came to England. On turning
a few pages I discover two poems I wrote
in Bengali, crafted in lines and curves so different
from the English script, beside notes I made
on the treatment of hernia and appendicitis.
The medical text now outdated but still clear.
I read the poems: the words spin and caress me,
a soft lullaby, and I'm spellbound by the sound,
the rhythm, and the music, a mantra in Sanskrit,
but couldn't understand what those words meant,
the poetic language of my birth has put on a veil
and won't communicate, a lover scorned. My
adopted language's severed the umbilical cord.

Transfusion

'Let me take you out for a treat.
It'll bring back fond memories,' she says.
They journey through dusty city roads.
The evening air fragrant with spicy smell,
those half-remembered days he spent
at home before leaving for England.
The destination, a large tin-roofed hall,
seating on matt-covered cement floor.
She quickly folds her legs under her
like a cat while he struggles.

Soon a sitar strings a few bars, Doogi Tabla
play 'Dhoom, Dhoom,' 'Tang, Tang.'
The harmonium's polished brown wood
glints under the stage light waiting for 'Ostad.'
Robed in flowing silk he enters, a king,
and then begins. His gold, diamond rings
sparkle as he caresses the bellow, his fingers
dance an Indian Waltz, his voice unfurls
an umbrella of sound. He teases the sitar,
dares the Tabla, both of them surrender like lovers.

On their way home they walk hand in hand
from the tram stop. She hums a tune from
the evening's concert. He joins in
opening his throat, his real coming home,
flushed with the music-blood of his past.

Joining up dots

The man with an audible limp used to sit
on the pavement at the end of our lane.
He sold lentils and rice stacked in front of him
like camel's humps. As a boy I used to go there
with grandpa to shop. They chatted about the war.
Grandpa would ask him how he lost his leg
in the Burma Campaign they both fought.
He weighed every item carefully, but no one
questioned the accuracy of his hand-held scale –
two metal dishes tied and suspended at the ends
of a short thick stick with coconut strings, and
crude weights. At sunset a friend would give him
a hand to roll up the worn jute-rug, pack the sacs
and load them into his cart. He'd head home
pushing the two-wheeler his wooden stump
thud-thudding on the tarmac.

Years on I go back. New houses and flats.
Shop windows display – *Sales* and *Bargains*.
I walk along the shiny concrete footpath
trying to locate the spot where he used to sit,
as if this way I could join up the dots
in my picture book and connect with the past.

Lost heirloom

My father kept a diary that nobody saw.
Rumour had it he wrote down 'secrets':
his romance, how he courted outside
his marriage, a poor clerk's son training
to become the best barrister in town,
his illness, real or faked, sons and daughters'
star-signs and birth dates, what he thought
about them, how he'd have really liked
to divide the inheritance. His drawers
were locked, no one had access and,
when he lay in bed dying no one had the heart
to ask him. We rummaged through his files,
books, desks but the diary never surfaced.
Now in my solitary moments I picture
in my mind what he's like – a young man
burning midnight oil to study hard, standing up
in court and arguing his cases before austere
white English judges, his love and adventure,
and finally the old man I well remember.
But what did he think of me? Really?
I wish I were at least a page in his diary.

Black shoes

'Men wear black shoes, boys brown,'
dad used to say to us many times.
That year I watched my older brother
get a pair of black leather shoes.
He polished them daily like a trophy.
I counted my birthdays and waited.
Finally thought at last this was my year.
I had seen a pair in the shopping arcade –
glistening under the window's strip light.
I drew a picture, and for special effect,
splashed darkest ink inside my lines
and one night slid the drawing under
mum and dad's bedroom door.
My friends brought cards and sweets.
We chatted, tossed about our wish lists.
But all the time my eyes kept drifting,
throat dried and heart raced wildly.
Mum brought a neatly wrapped box.
I held it firmly against my chest,
then opened my special birthday present:
a pair of leather shoes, shiny brown.

Flood

The burn behind our house swirled,
muddy water dragged down stream
fallen leaves like prisoners in a long chain.
Council workers handed out sandbags.
A new flood warning. 'How many bags
do you need?' Later sitting in the lounge
and drinking tea I thought about the flood
back home, a ten-year-old watching
from the verandah, our lane a mini Ganges.
Rain had poured bucketfuls for days.
People walked to work carrying their shoes
above head. Dad took a Rickshaw and
muttered about boys who missed schools
and played, rowing tubs and vessels,
makeshift boats, with sticks going up
and down. But I was grounded.
Today we put sandbags in the front
and move upstairs. No one's going to work.
We watched from our bedroom, water
splashing against the walls and doors,
calling me to come down and play
to make up for the lost fun of yesterdays.

The preacher and the shoppers

A small bald man in an old black suit waves
a Bible in the air. His voice resonates
round the city centre shops: 'Christ died
for our sin, the path to Lord is in giving
and not buying and amassing worldly things.'

A Geordie in a black and white strip listens
for a minute, then says to his mate, 'I wish
God would help United win the next match.'
Others throw cursory glances and move on.
Many filter in and out of department stores
carrying bulging bags. Some sit on benches
smoking, eating sandwiches and talking about
'Sales,' 'Bargains' while bored air drifts and
drags from concrete to glass.

Dusk falls, shops close, the preacher and
the shoppers go home. Tomorrow they'd
all be back, and two different worlds
would cross swords and live side by side.

Goodbye shoe doctor

The grey-haired man works in his shop
sitting in full view of the passers-by.
I bring an old pair of Swede shoes,
a birthday present from my late mum.
He takes a quick look, then puts them
on the floor, and carries on making
a new sole, measuring and cutting.
He holds the knife and incises like a surgeon
and hammers nails at precise distances,
adjusting and readjusting, a perfectionist.
On the shelves a display of shoes – white, black,
brown, red, children's, adults,' women's, men's,
flat heel, high heel, all with nametags;
'Some people, like you, care for their old shoes;
but most just throw them away.' He pauses.
'Yours would be ready in two days.' It's
as good as new when I collect mine. But
I realise then it'd be my last trip to this place –
there's a big sign on the door, 'Closing down.'

My thoughts

I open the front door.
A draft of cold air
sharp on my face.
The tarmac wet
from last night's rain.
The fir tree trembles
in February wind.
Brown leaves scatter
and lie limply on the lawn.

The cat next door hasn't
taken up its seat on the wall
between the two drives –
that unoccupied space,
an empty bed, shakes me.
I, in my dressing gown,
bend and pick up
the solitary bottle of milk.

Closing the door make
a cup of tea. I sip the drink
and think of you,
and those thoughts –
my cashmere shawl –
warm me, and freshen
the etching on the memory-plate.

A woman walks past me

She walks past me and smiles.
I feel a warmth, an un-seasonal spring.
After she'd gone I try to recall
that face: a neighbour, a friend,
a friend of a friend perhaps or
a patient I'd recently examined.
No, nothing fits. But the encounter,
the passing of two opposite trains,
lifts me, I feel weightless, unbound,
ready to float. I reach the bus stop –
let the first one go, then the second.
One or two cast suspicious glances –
'Who's he waiting for? Does he know
where he's going? Old fool!'
Finally I get on and show my bus pass.
I don't know where I'm heading,
still drunk with the sweet wine
of a stranger's unexpected smile.

My third soulmate

My first soulmate was rather soulless.
She would stop in the middle of a kiss
or a chat to look at her Blackberry or watch.
One day she sent an email, 'It's not working.'
And that's that.

The second soulmate burst into my life
like a hurricane, a blond with cat eyes
she was an athlete. But her muscular skill
and brain-dead wit got me paralysed,
we both wanted out. Her departing note
explained, 'Sorry sport, we are in different
leagues, and not playing the same game.'

The third soulmate came on the scene
via an accident – she was lying on the street,
had a few drinks, I nearly run her over.
But after a stomach-washout she sat up
in the ward, hugged me when I came to
visit her and said she loved me. Now we do
our own things – she to the pub and nightclubs
I to poetry Master-class. My friends worry.
But I know it's got to be third time lucky.

The life and time of Monty the spider

Monty the black spider
lived behind the radiator.
He was no fool.
He didn't like to be cold.

Every now and again
Monty ventured out in the open
in a series of stop-start
dance. But never for too long.
Because he didn't like to be cold.

One day he decided to go
for a long journey
and I watched him closely,
an irregular black spot
crawling and stopping
between carpet piles.

My wife didn't like creepy-
crawlies so I set a trap,
a folded newspaper
to whisk him away for good.

I lowered the edge of the device
and advanced with a steady hand.
He did an about turn/twist,
as if he read me, an open book,
and disappeared inside his den.
He didn't want to be cold.

Soon I forgot about the creature,
and he kept out of my sight.
One day, while Hoovering
I found him lying motionless,
his legs curled as if to keep warm
and his body a clump of DNA.

I took Monty out and buried him
in a shallow grave. I wrapped
a tin foil to insulate his coagulated
remains. He'd have loved that
because he never liked to be cold.

Don't bet on it

'I wish we'd won a lottery and gone on
a cruise, sunbathing and drinking.'
Or 'Why don't you get a proper job,
not a Council pen pusher, then we could
have holidays in Barbados?' Finally she said,
'You're a loser,' packed her bag and left.
He thinks of that remark as he picks up
the cheque – one million pound, a jackpot.
He'd to be ready soon for the local press,
and TV. How did he do it? He picked
a few numbers and watched them come good.
He looks at the zeroes on the cheque –
small bubbles; would they just float
and melt away? Is it all a dream?
No, she's been already on the phone,
cooing. He's told her to watch the Box.
The presenter asks what would he do
with the money. 'I'm not bothered.
It's my girl friend, she always wanted to go
on a world cruise, sunbathe and drink.
I'll wait for her and then plan.'
Then he turns round, winks and whispers,
'Don't bet on it, my sweetheart.'

Garbage

On radio John Humphrys interrogates
fiercely, 'Why is the Council bringing in
this extra charge when the Council tax
already sky high? Have you thought it out
clearly how the residents would react?
Not kindly I bet.' The councillor answers
defensively, 'John, John, listen. People are
throwing anything and everything in their bins.'
'So you propose to weigh ours and make us
pay heavily if we go over the quota set arbitrarily?'
'John, John, we've to recycle earnestly,
some, like you, do that regularly but many,
I'm sorry to say, act irresponsibly.'
John Humphrys clears his throat audibly,
'Suppose I put my rubbish into your bin,
would you pay for that or challenge me angrily?'
A long silence drops like a heavy curtain
abruptly. I switch off and sleep peacefully.

I was your Microwave

I remember the day you'd lifted me off
from the packing box onto the kitchen
worktop, your bride. Your eyes glazed staring
at my shiny white skin. I guessed you're
no cook. But you trusted me. I cooked
for you day and night, all you'd to do
is to pop in the ready meals – chicken curry,
Vindaloo, to name a few, the spiced aroma
danced as my plate turned – you feasted
on Sainsbury's sealed cuisine. But I used
to wait for the day you cleaned, your hand
caressed and wiped every corner of my body.
I shook like jelly. Then one day you put in
your mug of tea to heat, the liquid spun
and spewed choking me, soaking the circuit.
You dried me and changed the plug but
my heart won't start. Now you have a new one,
its touch-screen face sleek, many more features
and tricks. You'd soon be a Super-cook.
I'd be buried in the rubbish dump.
All I ask you to remember I wasn't just
a microwave, but much more than that.

A tasty meal

My name is Ben Nyambe.
I live in Kenya. I'm not a storyteller
but when you hear this account
I bet you'd be relieved that it's not you
but me, poor Ben, who's nearly swallowed.
That morning I was squatting under
a big oak tree (Toilets are few in the village
where I live) and humming a song 'Granny'
used to sing when I was a little boy.
Suddenly from nowhere a cold thick rope
circled round my chest tightening and
squeezing out my last breath. I shouted but
couldn't make any sound. Then I noticed
the monster anchored round the trunk had
opened it mouth trying to take me whole.
I'd a brainstorm, I found my mobile and rang 999.
At first they thought it's a joke. But thank god
for the bravery of our bobbies. They roped
the python and brought it down, and I survived.

PS: Police are now looking for that creature.
It escaped sliding under the cell door.
They want to put me up as the bait –
but I'm not rushing to volunteer!

A drunk discovers the buying power of a rag

Happy Hours! A crowd gather at the bar.
In a corner a middle-aged man sits,
his face red, eyes flushed, he's drinking
from his pint. Jim is a regular, he'd ask a
complete stranger, 'Would you buy me a pint?'
Some did. I pass him, buy a pint, return to my seat.
He doesn't approach me but his eyes focus
on my shoulders as I fetch and carry making two,
three trips. Finally I decide to leave, my head
a little dizzy. As I walk towards the door
I bump against a leg or a knee suddenly in the way,
and crash my head against an edge
and bleed, a spray. Jim is on the scene
like a flash and presses a rag hard on the cut,
it hurts, everything looks blurred. Later seated
on a chair, having my breath back I say,
'Thank you for most efficient First-aid.'
'Thank you, buying me drinks,' Jim responds.
'You deserve every glass.' Then he asks,
'Can I have my hanky back?' I hand him
the soiled cloth. He puts it in his pocket,
gets up, winks and says, 'You never know
when someone would need it next.'

Don't look

You want to look before you leap.
But how can you see what's there?
Is it gold you seek? But all that glitters...
You know the rest. You may suspend
your disbelief and discover a world
where future's an open book, and
all you need to do is to look, check up,
and jump cleanly over the hurdles.
But dreams don't end the way you want –
in real life safe landing's never guaranteed.
So give up the dream and be safe,
or go for it and leap, but don't look.

Mask

I like to change my skin-mask that'd clung
to me from birth. A baby can't remember
how it looked. It's face always 'cute.' Then
we grow. For a time mirrors humour us
winking at our designer haircut, the pencilled
eyebrows and the shaded eyes, the tweaked nose
and paper-white teeth. Soon they stop lying,
the landscape too deeply ploughed to be hidden –
just fold after fold of dead waves,
beyond the blade of the plastic surgeons.
But if only I could change it for one night,
if my mirror could lie for me once more,
even though I know change or no change
I'd still be the same, skin more than a mask.

Mumbai i The face

His face is all over the globe:
on TV screens, newspapers and magazines,
no crease in the skin, eyes looking
at CCTV and you and me
as if he hasn't a care in the world
he is about to turn upside down.
He had the same face, a little younger,
when he sat beside his mum
and got a hug before going to bed
after doing his homework,
listened to granddad telling stories –
how he fought in the war for Queen
who lived far away but was the ruler,
saw dad toil on rock-hard soil to grow
wheat and burley from a tiny plot.
He had the same face when he landed
with others on the city – the city
that danced that night like any other
with people, light, and traffic,
the city that promised a bundle of delight
to all, even to strangers like him.
But all along the face has hidden
a secret – it's not a face but a death-mask.

Mumbai ii 'Mum, I wet my pants'

'Mum, mum, I want to go for a wee.'
'Shush! Keep your voice down,'
she whispers. 'But mum...'
She tightens her arms around her
little girl huddled behind the sofa,
and stares towards the closed door
peering in the darkness. 'Mum...'
'Yes darling, soon.' A voice shouts,
'Please keep your daughter quiet.
Do you want all of us to be shot?'
Outside hurried footsteps, a cry,
a burst of automatic gunfire, then quiet,
only the sound of breathing, a moan
or two from twenty-odd hotel guests
packed like sardines on the floor.
'Mum I can't hold any more.'
'Shush! Shush! Shush! Shush!'
'Mum, I wet my pants.'

Mumbai iii Action Man

'Dad, do these men have guns like the soldiers?'
'I don't really know but I think so, son.'
'Are they soldiers, then, dad?'
'No, they are definitely not soldiers.'
'Why have they soldiers' guns then?'
'I can't tell you, son.'
'You gave me a gun on my birthday,
didn't you dad?'
'Oh, that's the Action Man and all
his gear. It's not the same.'
'But my gun makes rattling noises.
I played with Robin last weekend
hiding like we are doing today.'
A loud bang drowned their voices,
the door's ripped off, sound of cries, shouts,
running of feet, people falling, some trying
to get out of the room, some crouching.
'Dad, dad, my face hurts. Oh, it's wet.
Dad, I'm bleeding!' Dad doesn't speak.
The boy shakes him and utters a shrill cry.

Mumbai iv The wedding party

The party proceeds along the road
now cleaned of rubble, shards of glass,
abandoned shoes or bags, blood stains
washed, but one or two spots too stubborn
to erase and a few holes on the walls stare on.
The women wear glittering saris: red, orange,
blue and green, necklaces, bangles sparkle
in the evening light. Men don cream-silk Punjabi,
white suit, the bridegroom sits on a horse
his face made up with sandalwood paste,
a garland of marigold round the neck, musicians
march slowly in front beating Dhol (drum),
Bashiwalla playing the flute serenading the union.
Passers-by stop and watch, some click their cameras,
TV reporters do outside broadcast – 'The defiant city
carries on.' Many raise their glasses in the cafés.
A little distance away the 21-year-old locked up
in a secure cell wouldn't hear the music or
see the little parade – a couple beginning a new life.
But if he did, if he was on that street now
would he have fired his guns, hurled the grenades?

Two lives

1946. I was ten then. British Raj mortally wounded
but Hindu, Sikhs and Muslims at loggerhead.
I remember the scene outside our Kolkata flat,
a mob gliding along the tarmac like a hissing
giant snake, men with lathis and swords
shouting Allah-ho-Akbar. 'Come inside,'
mum whispering and tucking me in bed. Next day
I saw bodies lying in heaps in our playground.

2009. He was also ten when bullets bore holes
in his body as he came out to play with his friends
on the dusty rubble-strewn alley. 'Don't stay out long,'
mum had said, they'd been cooped up for days
as rockets after rockets had landed on the Strip.
Soon the tanks rolled in and snipers took aim.
They buried him with the other victims.
She crouched over the mound of earth and cried,
'I wish I was there to give you the last hug.'

Two lives, too young to understand
                              what's the price of freedom?

Arms and legs

                                    I have no legs.
I'd them when I went on foot patrol.
We'd been doing it for three months.
Through heat and dust. Young boys
followed us most days – for them it's like
watching live a scene from a movie
they'd heard of but not seen: soldiers
with rucksacks and guns. Many would come
closer, smile and one or two shout 'Hello,'
wink and hide. I'd wave, sometimes
we chatted, gave them chocolate. That day
I remember passing round a mound of earth
at the end of the winding village path. Suddenly
a deafening noise as if the world had exploded.
In my face. Now I know it wasn't the face.
I'd like to go on foot patrol again.

                                    But I have no legs.

                    ***   ***
                                    I have no arms.
I'd them when I punched the ball and
made a save. You see I won't let anyone score
against my team, we called ourselves Man United,
top of our local league. That evening
we're playing; a large silver bird came over us
from nowhere, and circled overhead.
It made a noise, like a lullaby, but not
what grandma hummed to put us to sleep,
it's scary. Then came the rockets, straight snakes
with fire in their tails whistling in and crashing
all round, thousand firecrackers. They couldn't
find my mum and dad. The nurse here is very kind.
She feeds me like my mum.
I wish I could play again in goal.

                                    But I've no arms.

What they said about the author's previous publications:

Chapati-Moon

'...Asit Maitra ... a [Emeritus] consultant at the RVI ... Newcastle ... has previously published poetry in Bengali. Chapati-Moon (ID on Tyne ...) this is his first collection in English. It begins with a childhood dream of visiting Britain and ends with a memory of growing up in Kolkata. In between are some lovely poems about the strangeness and the familiarity of both India and Britain, separated by "a flight path," but sleeping under the same "chapatti-moon."' - **Andy Croft, Morning Star (online),** Monday, 10 December 2007, POETRY: 21st Century Verse' December poetry releases

Sun Dips at Juhu Beach

'Asit takes a poetic look at his life,' **Evening Chronicle,** May 19, 2009

'THE DOCTOR

Having spent years dealing with people in stressful situations, former consultant Asit Maitra is now pouring his compassion into poetry...' **Sunday Sun,** June 21, 2009

'Continents collide in this engaging and moving collection from a distinguished A & E consultant turned poet.' **Other Poetry,** Series III, No. 4